ALLOSAURUS

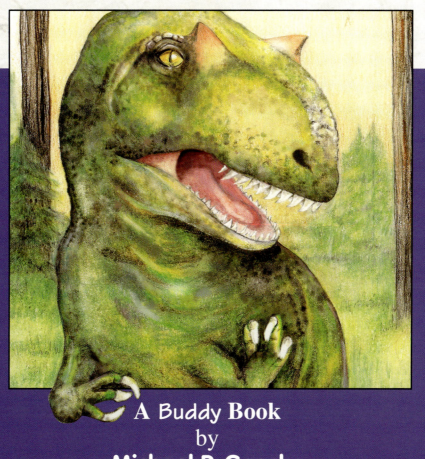

A Buddy Book
by
Michael P. Goecke

ABDO
Publishing Company

VISIT US AT

www.abdopub.com

Published by ABDO Publishing Company, 4940 Viking Drive, Edina, Minnesota 55435. Copyright © 2002 by Abdo Consulting Group, Inc. International copyrights reserved in all countries. No part of this book may be reproduced in any form without written permission from the publisher.

Printed in the United States.

Edited by: Christy DeVillier
Contributing editor: Matt Ray
Graphic Design: Denise Esner, Maria Hosley
Cover Art: Denise Esner, title page
Interior Photos/Illustrations: page 4: ©1999-2001 Christopher Srnka; pages 6 & 7: M. Shiraishi ©1999 All rights reserved; page 13: Julius Csotonyi; page 15: Patrick O'Brien; page 17: Tony Trammell; page 19: Bruce E. Shillinglaw; page 26: courtesy of the Peabody Museum at Yale University; page 27: courtesy of the Bureau of Land Management, Price, Utah.

Library of Congress Cataloging-in-Publication Data

Goecke, Michael P., 1968-
    Allosaurus/Michael P. Goecke.
      p. cm. – (Dinosaurs set II)
    Includes index.
    Summary: Describes the physical characteristics and behavior of the meat-eating dinosaur Allosaurus.
    ISBN 1-57765-636-9
    1. Allosaurus—Juvenile literature. [1. Allosaurus. 2. Dinosaurs.] I. Title.

QE862.S3 G59 2002
567.912—dc21

2001027931

TABLE OF CONTENTS

What Were They? 4

How Did They Move? 6

Why Was It Special? 8

Where Did It Live? 10

Who Else Lived There? 12

What Did They Eat? 16

Who Were Their Enemies? 18

Family Life 20

The Family Tree 22

Discovery 26

Where Are They Today? 28

Fun Dinosaur Web Sites 30

Important Words 31

Index 32

WHAT WERE THEY?

The Allosaurus was a large, meat-eating dinosaur. It was the biggest carnivore of the late Jurassic period. Carnivores eat meat.

Allosaurus
AL-uh-SOR-us

The great Allosaurus weighed about 4,000 pounds (1,814 kg). That is as heavy as a rhinoceros.

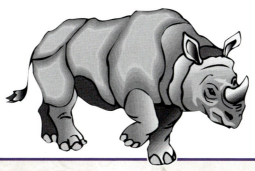

This dinosaur was about 38 feet (12 m) long. It stood almost 17 feet (5 m) tall. The Allosaurus's arms were small and short. It had three fingers on each hand. These fingers had sharp claws.

How did they move?

The Allosaurus walked on its two strong back legs. It could run about 20 miles (32 km) per hour. It was quick enough to catch animals to eat.

TAIL

LEG

FOOT

The Allosaurus held its tail straight behind it. This tail did not touch the ground.

WHY WAS IT SPECIAL?

The Allosaurus had a huge head. This head was about three feet (one m) long.

The great Allosaurus had a powerful mouth. This big dinosaur could eat 100 pounds (45 kg) of food in one bite. That is as much as four big turkeys.

An Allosaurus's tooth.

Tooth

Tooth Root

The Allosaurus had many teeth. They were shaped like sharp bananas. These teeth were three inches (eight cm) long.

Where Did It Live?

The Allosaurus mostly lived in North America. It lived about 150 million years ago. That was during the late Jurassic period.

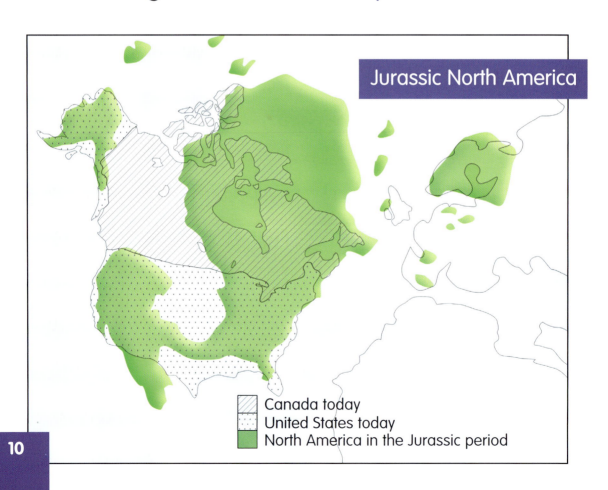

Jurassic North America

Canada today
United States today
North America in the Jurassic period

The Allosaurus's land was warm and wet. It was full of tropical forests. Sometimes, it rained a lot in these forests. The rainwater formed lakes.

Sometimes, it did not rain for a long time. This is a drought. These lakes turned into mud during a drought.

WHO ELSE LIVED THERE?

The Allosaurus lived with many sauropod dinosaurs. Sauropod dinosaurs have long necks. That is why we call sauropod dinosaurs "long necks."

The Diplodocus was a large plant-eating sauropod dinosaur. It had flat teeth in the front of its mouth. It swallowed plants whole.

The Diplodocus was a sauropod dinosaur.

The Allosaurus also lived among pterosaurs. Pterosaurs were reptiles that could fly. They had wings like bats. Some pterosaurs had wings that were 23 feet (7 m) long.

Most ptersosaurs were bigger than bats.

14

Pterosaurs could fly.

WHAT DID THEY EAT?

The meat-eating Allosaurus ate other dinosaurs. It ate the Diplodocus and other plant-eating dinosaurs.

The Allosaurus probably hunted and scavenged for food. Scavenging is eating an animal that is already dead.

The Allosaurus probably hunted other dinosaurs.

WHO WERE THEIR ENEMIES?

The Allosaurus was the meanest dinosaur at that time. No other dinosaur could equal its power. So, other dinosaurs stayed away from the Allosaurus.

Allosaursus dinosaurs were enemies of one another. They fought over food.

The Allosaurus fought each other for food.

FAMILY LIFE

Like a crocodile, the Allosaurus may have buried its eggs in the ground. The mother Allosaurus guarded these eggs. She guarded her babies, too. She took them to a special place.

Crocodiles take their babies to a crèche. A crèche is a safe place where baby crocodiles can hide. Maybe the Allosaurus took its babies to a crèche.

A crocodile crèche

THE FAMILY TREE

The Tyrannosaurus rex is a theropod dinosaur like the Allosaurus. Theropods stand on their back legs. They have sharp teeth. The T. rex lived millions of years after the Allosaurus.

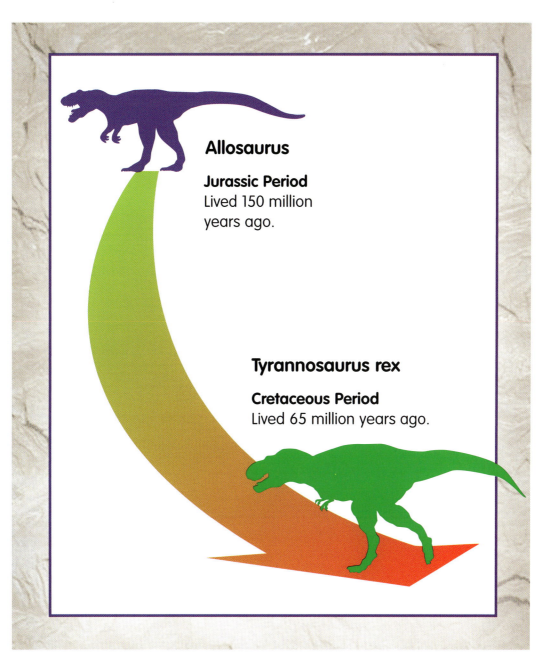

Allosaurus

Jurassic Period
Lived 150 million years ago.

Tyrannosaurus rex

Cretaceous Period
Lived 65 million years ago.

The T. rex and the Allosaurus were alike in many ways. Both dinosaurs were meat-eaters. They had big heads and teeth. Their arms were much smaller than their legs. The Allosaurus held its tail off the ground. So did the Tyrannosaurus rex.

Discovery

Othniel Charles Marsh named the Allosaurus. He found the first Allosaurus fossils near Morrison, Colorado in 1877.

Cleveland-Lloyd Quarry

Most Allosaurus fossils are from Cleveland-Lloyd Quarry in central Montana. This place was very muddy in the late Jurassic period. Paleontologists think the Allosaurus got stuck in this mud. Then, this mud saved the Allosaurus bones as fossils.

Where Are They Today?

Smithsonian National Museum of Natural History
10th Street and Constitution Avenue
Washington, D.C. 20560
www.nmnh.si.edu/paleo/dino

Royal Tyrrell Museum of Paleontology
Box 7500
Drumheller, Alberta T0J 0Y0 Canada
www.tyrrellmuseum.com

Brigham Young University Earth Science Museum
1683 North Canyon Road
Provo, Utah 84602-3300
cpms.byu.edu/ESM

Riverside Municipal Museum
3580 Mission Inn Avenue
Riverside, CA 92501
www.ci.riverside.ca.us/museum/

ALLOSAURUS

NAME MEANS	Different Lizard
DIET	Meat
WEIGHT	4,000 pounds (1,814 kg)
HEIGHT	17 feet (5 m)
TIME	Late Jurassic Period
ANOTHER THEROPOD	Tyrannosaurus rex
SPECIAL FEATURE	Big head
FOSSILS FOUND	USA—Colorado, Utah, Wyoming, Montana Australia, Tanzania, Portugal

The Allosaurus lived 150 million years ago.

First humans appeared 1.6 million years ago.

Triassic Period	Jurassic Period	Cretaceous Period	Tertiary Period
245 Million years ago	208 Million years ago	144 Million years ago	65 Million years ago

Mesozoic Era · Cenozoic Era

FUN DINOSAUR WEB SITES

Dinosaurs
www.cfsd.k12.az.us/~tchrpg/Claudia/Allo.html
Basic information about the Allosaurus, including behavior, habitat, and activities for children.

BBC Online – Walking with Dinosaurs
www.bbc.co.uk/dinosaurs/chronology/bigal
From the Discovery Channel series, "Walking with Dinosaurs," learn about the life of "Big Al." Read information about the life of an Allosaurus.

College of Eastern Utah Prehistoric Museum Home Page
www.ceu.edu/museum
Learn about the differences between the Allosaurus and the Tyrannosaurus rex. Read information about the Allosaurus being the grandfather of the T. rex.

The Riverside Municipal Museum presents the Allosaurus
www.ci.riverside.ca.us/museum/rmm/allo.html
Information about the Cleveland Lloyd Quarry and details on the anatomy of the Allosaurus.

IMPORTANT WORDS

carnivore a meat-eater.

dinosaur reptiles that lived on land 248-65 million years ago.

fossil remains of very old animals and plants.

Jurassic period a period of time that happened 208-146 million years ago.

North America one of the seven great land masses. The United States, Canada, and Mexico are in North America.

paleontologist someone who studies plants and animals from the past.

quarry a place where people dig into the ground to find things.

reptile an animal that breathes air, has scales, and lays eggs.

sauropod a kind of dinosaur that has a long neck, a long tail, and a small head.

tropical forest a warm and wet woodland.

Index

Australia, **29**

bat, **14**

carnivore, **4**

Cleveland-Lloyd Quarry, **27**

Colorado, **26, 29**

crèche, **20, 21**

Diplodocus, **12, 13, 16**

drought, **11**

eggs, **20**

fossil, **26, 27, 29**

Jurassic period, **4, 10, 23, 27, 29**

Marsh, Othniel Charles, **26**

Montana, **27, 29**

Morrison, Colorado, **26**

North America, **10**

Portugal, **29**

pterosaur, **14, 15**

reptile, **14**

sauropod, **12, 13**

scavenge, **16**

Tanzania, **29**

theropod, **22, 29**

tropical forest, **11**

Tyrannosaurus rex, **22-25, 29**

Utah, **29**

Wyoming, **29**